Held By The Moon, Kissed By You

Falling into Forever

Zaara Roohani

India | USA | UK

Dedication

To my family and my forever love,
For you are both the heart that shapes my soul.

Preface

In the dance of love, there are countless emotions—some fleeting, some eternal. As I poured my heart into these pages, I found myself torn between *two worlds*: the one that raised me with boundless affection, and the other that taught me the art of loving without limits.

This collection of poems unfolds the **stages of love**: the magnetic pull of **Dilkashi** (Attraction), the intoxicating surge of **Uns** (Infatuation), and the enduring beauty of **Mohabbat** (Love). With time, love deepens into **Aqidat** (Trust), a sacred bond, and blossoms into **Ibadat** (Worship), where it becomes a reverence. But love is not without its madness—**Junoon** (Madness)—which drives us to the edge. And at its most profound, love leads to **Maut** (Death), where all is surrendered and merged into eternity.

These poems are not just words on paper, but fragments of my soul, captured in moments of bliss and heartache. I dedicate them to my family, whose love is my foundation, and to the one who holds my heart, a love that knows no boundaries.

To the reader, I invite you to immerse yourself in the beauty and pain of love as I have, and perhaps find a piece of your own story within these verses.

Acknowledgements

First and foremost, I thank **God**, whose blessings have danced through my life like fairy kisses. Without their gentle guidance, none of this would have been possible, and I'm forever grateful for His divine presence lighting every step of this journey.

To my **family**, especially my **amma** and **appa**—you are the *heartbeat* of everything I do. Your love, support, and faith in me have been my greatest strength. You've taught me to dream, to work hard, and to love deeply. I owe everything to you both. I can't express enough how much your love means to me and that I love you much more.

To my **forever love**—you have been my muse, my inspiration, and the reason I believe in love that knows *no boundaries*. Your love fills the pages of this book, and *I dedicate every verse to you*. I am endlessly grateful for the way you love me, and I carry that love in every line I've written.

Cheers to my **friends**—thank you for being my constant companions, my cheerleaders, and my safe space. You've seen me through the highs and the lows, always offering your wisdom, laughter, and support. This book is as much yours as it is mine, because it's your friendship that's helped me find my voice.

I am deeply grateful to **BookLeaf Publishing** for this wonderful opportunity and for providing a platform where my words could find a home. Your support and dedication to writers like me make dreams turn into reality. Thank you for believing in my voice and giving me the space to share my journey with the world.

And to everyone who believed in me, supported me, and patiently waited for me to finish—thank you from the bottom of my heart. This book is a *piece of my soul*, and I hope you find a part of yours within its words.

1. Dilkashi - Meeting of eyes

Uski aankhon ki dilkashi, ek naya afsana ban gayi,
Narmi bhari wo nazar, mere dil ke gehrayon tak samayi.
Pehli mulaqat ka jaadu, ab tak mehsoos hota hai,
Har dafa jo dekha usse, ek nayi roshni si chhayi.

The allure in his eyes wove a story so pure,
His tender gaze, a depth my heart could not ignore.
The enchantment of that first meeting lingers still,
Each glance at him, a light that time can't still.

2. Dilkashi - A connection

Muskurahaton mein taraasha ek rishta gulon jaisa,
Waqt ke saath khilta raha, mehka sada jaisa.
Be-awaaz ek samajh, taqdeer ki lehar thi,
Jab mile hum, ban gaye ek doosre ke humsafar thi.

A bond woven in smiles, so gentle, so true,
Blooming with time, like the morning dew.
A silent connection, a fate intertwined,
When we met, our souls aligned.

3. Dilkashi - Magnetic Pull

Hawa mein dilkash afsana likha tha,

Uski nigahon ne mujhe bechain sa kar diya.

Ek jhilmilati nazar, bijli si gir gayi,

Jaise kashish ne mujhe uske hawale kar diya.

The air had woven a tale so divine,

His gaze, a spell, made my heart entwine.

A single glance, like a storm's embrace,

As if destiny pulled me to his space.

4. Uns - Mesmerized

Ek naam tha, naghma ban gaya,
Be-awaaz sa tha, saathi ban gaya.
Uski baatein hawaon mein gunjti rahi,
Har mehfil mein ek dastaan bani.
Kya woh guzarati hawa tha, ya toofaan mera?
Jise panah samajh, khudko mitane laga?

His name was a whisper, now a song,
An unspoken tune I've known all along.
His words, like echoes, refused to fade,
Carved in the wind, in memories they stayed.
Was he a passing breeze, or the storm I mistook for
home?
A touch so deep, I made it my own.

5. Uns - Whispers of doubt

5

Mujhe darr tha, saath nibhana tha,
Sirf ek lamha nahi, zindagi ka fasana tha.
Uski baahon mein ek jahaan tha,
Magar dil ka raaz bhi wahan tha.
Manzoori ek taraf, mohabbat ek jaan,
Kya chunu, rishta ya armaan?

I feared, for I longed to stay,
Not just a moment, but forever this way.
In his arms, a world so divine,
Yet in my heart, a secret confined.
Family on one side, love on the other,
Do I choose duty or remain his forever?

6. Uns - Hope and Fate

Na sirf dilkashi, na sirf ek pal ka jadoo,
Uske lafzon mein ek meharbani thi.
Woh ek saaya tha, jo mujhe sambhalne laga,
Har jazba ab ek gehri chaahat bani.

Not just a spark, nor a fleeting sigh,
But a warmth that wrapped me, safe and tight.
In his voice, a softness, in his gaze, the sky,
And what was once a passing dream, turned infinite.

7. Mohabbat - Untold Love

Ek pal mein taqdeer sanwar gayi,
Halki si baat, mohabbat ubhar gayi.
Jo sirf ek jhalak thi, gehra asar ban gayi,
Bezubaan thi mohabbat, magar amar ho gayi.

In a breath, the stars realigned,
A whisper of fate, so softly entwined.
What was a spark, now endlessly grew,
A love unspoken, yet perfectly true.

8. Mohabbat - Confession

Tum aaye toh jazbaat mehke sanam,
Bekhabar dil bhi tere geet kehne laga.
Bas baatein hi kaafi thi saari duniya ke liye,
Tera waqt mil jaaye, toh aur kya chahiye?

Like a whisper, you stole my name,
My heart surrendered, lost in your flame.
In fleeting moments, love took its flight,
And your presence became my endless light.

9. Mohabbat - Falling softly

Teri chaahaton mein kho rahi hoon,
Har saans teri ho rahi hoon.
Agar tu chahe toh bikhar bhi jaaun,
Tere labon ki nami mein pighal bhi jaaun.
Mohabbat mein teri fanaa ho jaaun,
Bas ek baar mujhme samaa toh jaaun.

In your love, I lose myself,
With every breath, I become yours.
If you wish, I will fall apart,
Melt in the warmth of your whispered touch.
Let me vanish in the depths of you,
Just once, let me belong to you.

10. Aqidat - Fated Love

Chaha nahi, bas tujhe chun liya maine,
Har raah mein tera hi raasta liya maine.
Taqdeer pe yaqeen hai, par ikhtiyar bhi tha,
Teri mohabbat ko dil ka qarar diya maine.
So jahan bhi dekhun, tera chehra mile,
Har janam, har lamha, tera saath chun liya maine.

I did not fall, I chose to stay,
In every step, you lit my way.
Fate may write, but hearts decide,
And mine found home by your side.
In every life, in every dream,
I'd choose you still, in love serene.

11. Aqidat - A Glow of Trust

Teri baaton mein jo sukoon mila,
Woh sajda hai meri duaon ka.
Har mod pe tera saath chaha,
Jaise chaand ho raaton ka.
Mujhko khud se bhi zyada yakeen hai,
Meri rooh hai teri panaahon ka.

In your words, I found my peace,
A prayer answered with gentle ease.
At every turn, I wished for you,
Like the moon that lights the midnight hues.
I trust you more than I trust my own,
For my soul is yours, my heart your home.

12. Aqidat - Forever shine

Tera yakeen tha, jo raah dikhane laga,
Ishq ka deepak, roshni barsane laga.
Har shab tere naam ki ibaadat hui,
Meri ruh teri mohabbat ki aadat hui.
Ab sirf pyaar nahi, ek bandagi hai,
Tera saath meri sabse badi daulat rahi.

Your trust once lit the path so true,
Like a silent flame, it softly grew.
Love turned to worship, pure and deep,
A sacred vow my soul will keep.
No longer just love, but a faith divine,
In your arms, forever, let me shine.

13. Ibadat - Longing

Teri ibaadat mein kho gaye hum,
Har saans mein bas tu hi tu hai sanam.
Aankhon ne dekha roshni tera noor,
Dil ne sajaya tujhe har dastoor.
Meri mohabbat sirf ek sajda bani,
Tujhse judaa ho yeh himmat kahan?

Lost in the worship of you, my love,
Every breath whispers your name above.
My eyes behold your radiant light,
My heart adores you, pure and bright.
My love has become a sacred prayer,
To part from you—I wouldn't dare.

14. Ibadat - The Surrender

Teri duaon mein basa hoon main,
Teri roshni ka sila hoon main.
Har saans tujhe apna kar di,
Har dukh pe tera naam likh diya.
Mera ishq sirf ek sajda bana,
Teri chahat meri taqdeer bana.

I have carved your name in my soul,
With every heartbeat, you take control.
In your shadow, my world feels bright,
Your love turns darkness into light.
No path exists where you're not near,
In every life, I'll seek you, my dear.

15. Ibadat - Moon and Love

15

Ishq karo toh shab ke saaye ki tarah,
Chand ki roshni bhi, uski tanhaayi bhi gawarah.
Har zakham ko mohabbat ka gehna samajh lo,
Har dukh ko apni wafa ka sajda kar do.
Na shikayat ho, na koi guzarish rahe,
Bas ek naam ho, ek ibaadat rahe.

Love like the night, silent and deep,
Embrace the moon, yet its shadows keep.
Let every wound be an ornament divine,
Let every sorrow in devotion shine.
No pleas, no wishes, just a sacred call,
One name, one worship, and that is all.

16. Junoon - Obsession

Tera zikr ho toh dil deewana ho jaye,
Har saans tujhe sajda karne ko chahe.
Meri raaton ka chand sirf tu hi toh hai,
Teri roshni mein hi jeene ki chaah hai.
Ishq mera koi dastaan nahi bas ibadat hai,
Har dhadkan tujhme samaane ki aadat hai.
Main baarish ban kar tere lab chho loon,
Ya hawa ban ke tujhme kho jaoon.
Meri deewangi ka koi shumar nahi,
Tere bina duniya ka koi ikraar nahi.
Main fanaa ho jaoon teri ek nigah pe,
Bas tera ho jaane ki guzarish hai.

Your name is carved in the echoes of my breath,
Without you, love is an illusion, a hollow death.
I do not live; I merely exist in your grace,
Drunk on your touch, lost in your embrace.
If love is a fire, let me burn without fear,
Let me drown in your soul, crystal clear.
I'd break the heavens to hold you near,
Steal every fate just to keep you here.
You are not just love—you are divine,
A madness, a worship, forever mine.
Even if the world fades, I swear,
I will find you, in life or in air.

17. Junoon - Burning desire

Teri ungliyon ka safar meri gardan pe,
Aag bhadkaaye jaise shabnam ke badan pe.
Teri saansein uljhi hain mere zulfon mein,
Main qaid hoon tere bechain honton mein.
Meri chaadar bhi teri khushbu se mehkaaye,
Teri chhup chhup ke choone ki aadat sulgaaye.
Har lamha tere ishq ka nasha chadhaaye,
Zuban pe tera naam madhosh kar jaaye.
Tujh mein kho ke main khud se begana hoon,
Tere honton pe rakh ke saansein deewana hoon.
Yeh raat, yeh badan, yeh junoon ka safar,
Sirf tu, sirf main, aur ishq ka asar.

Your fingers trace rivers down my skin,
Like fire melting the frost within.
Your breath tangles deep in my hair,
I'm trapped in the hunger we share.
My sheets still whisper your name,
Your stolen touches set me aflame.
Every moment, your love's sweet ache,
Drunk on you, I shiver and break.
Lost in you, I forget who I am,
Breathing you in, drowning like sand.
This night, this heat, this burning desire,
Only you, only me, only wildfire.

18. Junoon - Restless

Dil beqarar, junoon bepanah,
Teri chaahat mein kho gaya raah.
Har lamha tujhe mehsoos karun,
Teri saanson mein bas ke jeeya karun.
Labon ki pyaas, teri baatein bujhaye,
Hathon ki lakeerein sirf tujh tak jaayein.
Aankhon mein teri jo nasheeli shabnami,
Us mein doob ke khud ko bhool jaaye.
Main hoon ya nahi, bas tu hi tu hai,
Ibadat bhi tu, ishq bhi tu hai.
Teri chaahaton ka yeh junoon hai ya sukoon?
Mujhe khud se bhi ab hai fursat kahaan!

My heart aches, my love untamed,
In your desire, all paths seem unnamed.
Each moment, I feel you near,
Living in the breath you whisper here.
The thirst on my lips, your words subdue,
The lines on my palms, all lead to you.
Your eyes, like wine, drenched in night,
Drown me deep, lost in their light.
Am I myself, or just your trace?
You are my worship, my sweetest embrace.
Is this love a madness or peace so divine?
I've no time for myself—only you in my mind.

19. Maut - Attachment

Tere bina saansein bhi bojh lagti hain,
Jee kar bhi main bas mar si rahi hoon.
Mitti sa badan, rooh bhi khaali,
Tere bina main bas dhool si udi hoon.
Chand bhi be-noor, raat bhi andheri,
Meri mehfil ab tanhaaiyon se bhari.
Tere bina har mehsoos be-asar,
Jaise darya ho par paani na ho andar.
Meri baahon ki lakeerein sirf tujhe dhoondhe,
Par haath sirf khaali hawaa pakde.
Agar tu na ho, toh kuch bhi nahi,
Mohabbat bhi bas ek kahani suni.

Without you, even breath feels heavy,
Living, yet dying, lost and unsteady.
A body of dust, a soul left hollow,
Drifting like ashes, with nowhere to follow.
The moon is dim, the night is blind,
Loneliness lingers where love once shined.
Without you, all touch feels numb,
Like rivers that flow, yet lifeless they run.
My arms trace lines that lead to you,
Yet grasp only air, empty and blue.
If you're not here, then nothing remains,
Love itself just a story in vain.

20. Maut - Pain

Meri aadat ho, meri ehsaas ho,
Har baat ka ek alfaaz ho.
Tera chalna, tera rukna seekh liya,
Teri tarah jeena, marna seekh liya.
Par agar ek din tu chhod gaya,
Main bikharta mitti sa ho jaunga.
Mohabbat ka yeh junoon ab sawaal hai,
Tera hona hi toh mera haal hai.
Tere bina zindagi sirf dukh banegi,
Har pal ek naya maut ka zakham degi.
Teri yaadon ka zehar rag rag mein bharega,
Main jeeta rahunga, par har roz marunga.

You are my habit, my very soul,
A word born from the stories told.
I learned to walk the way you do,
To breathe, to love, to die like you.
But if one day, you drift away,
Like dust in the wind, I'll fade away.
This love, this madness—now a curse,
Your presence alone defines my universe.
Without you, life is an endless ache,
Each moment, a wound that will never break.
Your memories, like poison, run through my veins,
I'll live, but die a thousand deaths in pain.

21. Maut - Seperation

Meri mohabbat kisi saude ka naam nahi,
Teri chaahat ke bina zindagi ek daag sahi.
Ya toh tu ho, ya sirf khaali khaali raaste,
Saans bhi le lu toh lagay jaise saza ke vaaste.
Agar tere bina jeena likha hai taqdeer mein,
Toh behtar hai mitt jana kisi shab-e-seher mein.
Maut ka dukh bhi teri judai se halka hoga,
Har boond khoon ki bas tera naam pukarega.
Par kahin aasmaan ke kisi aakhri mod pe,
Mujhe milna tu ik nayi kahani ki godh pe.
Main rooh banke bhi teri baahon ka intezaar karunga,
Tere bina har janam adhoora guzara karunga.

My love is not a bargain to be lost,
Without you, life itself is a grieving ghost.
Either you stay, or emptiness remains,
Even breathing feels like a cruel chain.
If fate has written my days without you,
Then I'd rather vanish into the sky's quiet blue.
Even death would hurt less than this pain,
Every drop of blood would still call your name.
But somewhere beyond the stars' last light,
Find me again in a love born right.
Even as a soul, I'll wait in despair,
For without you, no life is ever fair.